Animal Secrets

John Townsend

Published in association with The Basic Skills Agency

Hodder & Stoughton

A MEMBER OF THE HODDER HEADLINE GROUP

Acknowledgements
Cover: Barry Downard

Photos: p 5 © NHPA/NORBERT WU; p 11 © Corbis; p 27 © John Cancalosi/Still Pictures.

Illustrations: Chris Coady

Every effort has been made to trace copyright holders of material reproduced in this book. Any rights not acknowledged will be acknowledged in subsequent printings if notice is given to the publisher.

Orders; please contact Bookpoint Ltd, 130 Milton Park, Abingdon, Oxon OX14 4SB. Telephone (44) 01235 827720, Fax: (44) 01235 400454. Lines are open from 9.00–6.00, Monday to Saturday, with a 24 hour message answering service. You can also order through our website www.hodderheadline.co.uk

British Library Cataloguing in Publication Data
A catalogue record for this title is available from the British Library

ISBN 0 340 87143 1

First published 2003
Impression number   10 9 8 7 6 5 4 3 2 1
Year   2007 2006 2005 2004 2003

Copyright © 2003 John Townsend

Typeset by SX Composing DTP, Rayleigh, Essex.
Printed in Great Britain for Hodder & Stoughton Educational, a division of Hodder Headline, 338 Euston Road, London NW1 3BH by The Bath Press, Bath.

Contents

1 Introduction

Animals have hidden powers.

Secrets.

Humans are only just finding out about some of them.

Some secrets may take years to find yet.

You may think people are clever.

You may think we are top of all animals.

Humans have all the best skills.

We make music.

We paint pictures.

We build great works of art.

Our brains are the best of all.

Just think of all the things we can do.

Yet now and again animals surprise us.

They can even make us look dull.

They can do some things

we can only dream about.

Do you know a bee can give a map-dance?

Do you know some fish do not freeze?

Do you know some lizards shoot blood from their eyes?

Do you know some pets 'cry' over their owners?

Do you know some animals can see the future?

You'll be amazed.
The animal world is full of secrets . . .

2 Electric

This may shock you.
Some fish pack a punch that can knock you flat.
They can pump out enough volts to stun a horse.
Some can even kill you.
That's quite a zap!

Electric eels live in South America.
They can shoot out up to 600 volts.
It's to stun their prey.
It can kill some people.

How does the eel do it?
It has electric cells in its tail.
They slowly charge up.
It's like a big battery.
This energy also helps to guide the eel in murky water.
But that's where it's easy to step on one.
All three metres of it.
Ouch!
(A bit like poking your toe in the light socket!)

Many seafish can give shocks as well.
But it's not often very much.
The electric ray can make up to 200 volts.
The shock comes from a big fin by each eye.
In Roman times they used the ray
to treat a headache.
They put the fish on your head
and let it spark!
It was meant to cure a bad head.
It didn't always work.
It didn't do the fish much good, either!

The electric catfish lives in Africa.
It can grow to over a metre long.
You can't keep it in a tank, though.
It will kill all the other fish.
One quick zap and they'll all die of shock.
It can pump out up to 350 volts at a time.
That could be handy in a power cut!
How does it do it?
It's still something of a secret.
Just another wonder of nature.

An electric catfish has a kick like an electric fence.

3　On the Move

Some animals, birds and fish travel for miles.
They may cross the world.
Some stay in groups.
Some travel on their own.
They go to find food, a home or a mate.
But there's a big question.
How do they know where to go?
Why don't they get lost?
Just how do they do it?

People get lost all the time.
Most of us know what it's like to lose our way.
Have you ever tried to get out of a maze?
Could you find your way home
from the other side of the world?
Some animals can do just that.

Some geese have a sixth sense.
They use the Earth's magnetic force
to find their way.
So do pigeons.
They can fly home from anywhere.
They don't need a map.
It's just instinct.

Animals are on the move all the time.
Some migrate hundreds of miles.
They go on huge journeys.
They meet danger all the time.
But they never give up.
They just know they have to go.
It's no holiday, however.
It can be a case of life or death.

Some pets have been on secret travels.
Their stories may surprise you.
Just how do cats and dogs know where to go?

A family moved from Wisconsin to Arizona in 1986.
That's 2400 kilometres.
They took their cat, Sam, with them.
A year later they moved back to Wisconsin.
This time they left Sam behind.
Guess what? Sam felt lonely.
He had plans.
Four years later in Wisconsin,
the family heard a noise at the door.
They took a look outside and there he was.
Sam had come back.
All on his own.
That's quite a hike.

How do they do it?

Some dogs baffle the experts.
They track down their owners for long distances.
In 1923, Bobbie got lost.
He was a collie.
He was 5,000 kilometres from home.
Six months later he turned up.
Back home.
He'd crossed rivers and mountains.
He was a bit thin, but it was Bobbie all right.
There was no doubt about it.

A cat finds its way home after a long journey.

In 1979, another dog got lost.
Nick was in the Arizona desert.
She was 3,000 kilometres from home.
Somehow she found her way back.
It took four months.
It was 3,000 kilometres across open country.
She had to cross rivers and mountains.
She had to get across the Grand Canyon.
Even a soldier with a compass and radio
would find that tough, but not Nick.
She got back to the doorstep
with a bark and a wag of her tail.
Amazing!

No one can be really sure
how animals do this.
Is it an extra sense?
Is it an unseen power?
Can some pets tune in to their owner's mind?
Maybe they know more than we think.
Spooky!

The Dog that Swam for Miles

In 2002, a dog fell off a boat into the sea.

His name was Todd.

His owner looked for him for hours.

They were 1.5 kilometres away from the Isle of Wight,

but Todd's home was the other way.

It was fifteen kilometres across the sea

and up river, so that's just where he went!

Todd swam fifteen kilometres across choppy sea.

After six hours, he walked on to dry land.

He was a fit dog and knew he had to get home.

That took some doing, and it's quite clever, too!

His owner was over the moon.

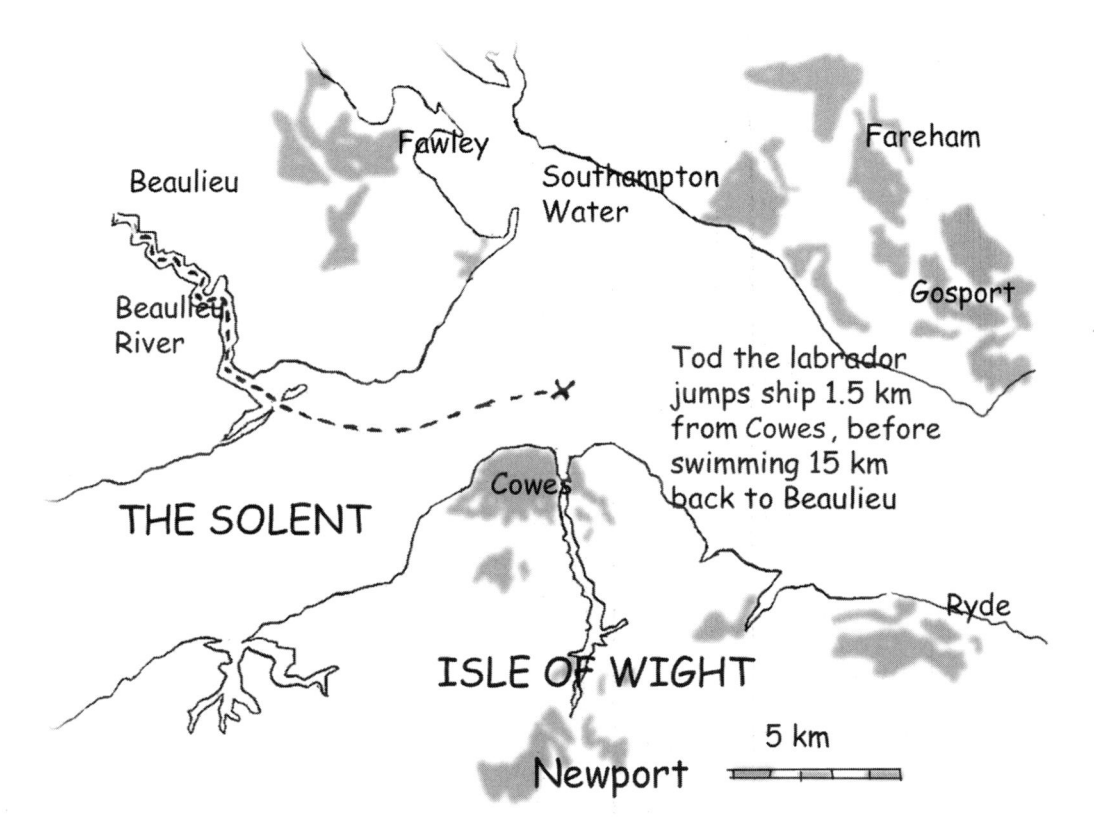

Beaulieu

Fawley

Southampton
Water

Fareham

Beaulieu
River

Gosport

Tod the labrador
jumps ship 1.5 km
from Cowes, before
swimming 15 km
back to Beaulieu

THE SOLENT

Cowes

Ryde

ISLE OF WIGHT

5 km

Newport

Todd's journey.

4　Saying 'Hello'

Why are people so clever?

What makes us different from animals?

The anwer is, we can talk.

We can tell other people all sorts of things.

For years we thought animals were dumb.

Now we know it's not true.

Animals can say far more than 'Hello' . . .

Chatty Birds

Many pet birds can say a few words.

They learn to repeat sounds.

But can they really talk?

Some people think birds know

what they are saying.

Some budgies can say up to 500 words.

They can repeat poems, too.

A parrot once said 800 words.

That's a lot of talking.

But can creatures tell us what they *think*?

Insect Talk

Insects can 'talk', too.
Some are good at telling others about food.
Or danger.
Even tiny ants get their message across.
If one finds food it will let others know.
It may be the way it moves. Or a sound.
It may be sign language.
Somehow it talks.
In seconds the swarm will be on the move.
Bees are clever, too.
A bee can tell the rest of the hive all sorts of things.
How does it do it?
Not by 'talking', but with a dance.
And a buzz with a wiggle.
That's how it tells all its friends
where the best pollen is.
Each move tells them just where to fly. Like a map.
It even tells them where to turn left and right.
How clever is that?

Under Water

In the last few years we've found out
about sounds under the sea.
Whales can 'sing' for hours at a time.
The tune can go high and low.
Some make lots of 'clicks'.

Dolphins seem to whistle. Why?
It's to tell other dolphins what's going on.
It's like their own language.
They can talk over very long distances.
There's still a lot to find out.
We don't know yet how these underwater sounds
really work.

One day . . .

People have taught apes to talk.
They use sign language or a system of grunts.
Some apes have learned how to ask
for different things.

Apes in the wild have their own way of 'talking'.
A high grunt means one thing.
A low grunt means another.
People have tried to work out what the grunts mean.
They have tried to talk back to the apes.
There's far more to ape talk
than we once thought.
One day, we may learn to have
a real chat with a chimp.

It goes to show that humans aren't
the only ones who can talk.
We know that now.
We once called them 'dumb animals'.
It may not be long before they answer us back!

5 Helping Paws

Can animals care?
Do they have feelings?
Can they understand?
They do in stories.

Just think of Lassie. Or maybe Scooby Doo!
Dogs rush to the rescue in a lot of stories.
On TV, a clever dolphin saves the day.
Or a horse or a kangaroo.
They save the hero just in time!
But these are just stories.
Can animals really tell when we need help?
Can they really save lives?
Do animals sense danger?
Some people think they do.

This story hit the news in 2002.
It told of a seal that saved a dog.
What do you think?

SEAL SAVES DOG

A dog fell in the River Tees.
The fast current swept it into deep water.
It soon began to drown.
Mr Hinds was walking on the bank.
He saw that the dog was in trouble.
He phoned the RSPCA.

The dog gave a yelp.
Just then a seal popped up in the river.
It swam round the dog and pushed it with its nose.
It got the dog to a mud bank.

Mr Hinds said, 'I couldn't believe my eyes.
I was sure the dog was about to drown.
It took just a few seconds for the seal to save the dog.
I don't know why the seal did it!'

When the RSPCA arrived, the dog was on dry land.
Three other seals were nearby in the river.
They were keeping a close eye on him.
The RSPCA said, 'The dog owes its life to the seal.'

Dolphins to the Rescue

Dolphins have helped people for years.
The Greeks told stories of dolphins
coming to the rescue.
Many times they've saved humans from death.

There are reports of dolphins
saving people from sharks.
They've chased off sharks that bite divers.
A dolphin will call others to come and help.

In 1997, a woman was in trouble
under the sea off South Africa.
Five dolphins swam to help her.
They lifted her to the surface.
Then they took her back to the shore.
She was amazed!

Does your pet care about you?

A news story from 2001 said:

DOG'S LOVE BITE KILLS OWNER
A woman had a fit in her home.
Her dog tried to help her.
Kirsty Ross was found dead with cuts to her neck.
At first the police thought her dog attacked her.
Later they worked out what happened.
Her dog tried to lift her up
to help her breathe.
It tried to lift her by her clothes,
but that didn't work.
Then it held her by the neck,
just how a dog holds its puppy.
The dog was trying so hard that the bite killed her.

How loyal is your dog?
If you left, would it be upset?
We don't know much about our pets' feelings.

John Gray was an old man.
His dog Bobby was two years old in 1858.
Sadly John died, and Bobby was full of grief.
He wouldn't leave his dead master.
Every night for the next fourteen years,
Bobby slept on John's grave.
When he died, Bobby was buried with his master.
People still go to see the grave in Edinburgh.
It's a famous story of a dog's love for his owner.

Hachi Ko lived with his master in Japan.
Every night Hachi Ko ran to meet his master
off the train.
The dog was always there on time.
But in 1925, his master died at work.
He never came back on the train.
Hachi Ko got a new owner, but he never gave up.
Every night for the next ten years,
the dog went to the station.
He sat and waited.
Hachi Ko was a hero.
When he died they built a statue at the station.

How did Moggie Know?

In 1974, a cat called Moggie made the news.
Her owner was an old lady.
She had to go into hospital, and sadly she died.
The next day Moggie vanished.

The funeral was 16 kilometres away.
Just as the old lady's coffin went into the grave,
Moggie turned up.
The cat sat beside the open grave.
She had never been there before.
How did she know where to go?
Did she sense where her dead owner was?

This is just one more case
of a pet showing feelings.
How do you explain it?
Maybe there's more to our pets than meets the eye.

6 Did You Know?

Nature is full of surprises.
Did you know any of these strange facts?

• The flying squirrel has loose flaps of skin.
  These turn it into a hang-glider
  when it leaps from a tree at night.
  It can fly from tree to tree like Superman!

• The Alaska black fish can live in very icy water.
  Not much can live at $-20°C$.
  That's colder than a frozen kipper!

• Other fish (like the pupfish) can live in hot water.
  In fact, some parts of the sea make steam.
  Vents from deep in the earth can boil the water.
  A worm lives in this water at $80°C$.
  Ouch!

- What do you do if people annoy you?
  Just think if you could give them a stare
  till your eyes shot blood in their face.
  A good trick!
  That's just what a horned toad lizard does
  to scare its enemy.
  Jets of blood squirt from its eyes –
  over a metre into the air.
  That's enough to make anyone run!

A Regal Horned Lizard.

- Many reports tell of pets sensing danger.
  Some dogs know if an earthquake is on its way.
  In World War Two,
  there was a bad bomb raid in Exeter.
  A few hours before, cats left the city.
  People saw them get up and go.
  It's as if they knew what was coming.
  How did they know?

Some secrets we may never find out.
The animal world is full of them.
Puzzles. Mystery.

We've known about some animal secrets
a long time.
We are only finding answers now, though.
There is still so much to learn.
Will we ever know about all the creatures
that share our planet?
They seem to have more secrets
than we ever knew.
You could say animals are nothing less
than super-human after all!